How to Draw the Life and Times of
John Adams

Ryan P. Randolph

The Rosen Publishing Group's
PowerKids Press™
New York

To my dad, William Randolph

Published in 2006 by The Rosen Publishing Group, Inc.
29 East 21st Street, New York, NY 10010

First Edition

Editor: Rachel O'Connor
Layout Design: Ginny Chu

Illustration Credits: All illustrations by Holly Cefrey
Photo Credits: pp. 4, 14 Courtesy of the Massachusetts Historical Society; p. 7 © Museum of Fine Arts, Boston, Seth K. Sweetser Fund/Bridgeman Art Library; pp. 8 (statue), 9, 16 (Boston Massacre), 22, 24 (print, flag), 26 Library of Congress Prints and Photographs Division; p. 10 Courtesy of the Adams National Historic Site, National Park Service; p. 12 Ginny Chu; p. 16 (teapot) Colonial Williamsburg Foundation; p. 18 Rosen Publishing; p. 20 Courtesy USS BOSTON Shipmates, Inc., http://www.uss-boston.org, painting © James A. Flood; p. 28 U.S. Senate Collection.

Library of Congress Cataloging-in-Publication Data

Randolph, Ryan P.
How to draw the life and times of John Adams / Ryan P. Randolph.— 1st ed.
    p. cm. — (A kid's guide to drawing the presidents of the United States of America)
Includes bibliographical references and index.
ISBN 1-4042-2979-5 (library binding)
1. Adams, John, 1735–1826—Juvenile literature. 2. Presidents—United States—Biography—Juvenile literature. 3. Drawing—Technique—Juvenile literature. I. Title. II. Series.

E322.R36 2006
973.4'4'092—dc22

                                    2004014561

Manufactured in the United States of America

Contents

1 Meet John Adams 4

2 The Second President 6

3 John Adams's Massachusetts 8

4 Childhood and Family 10

5 The Education of John Adams 12

6 Love and Marriage 14

7 The Stamp Act 16

8 The American Revolution 18

9 John Adams Becomes a Diplomat 20

10 First Vice President of the United States 22

11 Peace with France 24

12 The Presidential Election of 1800 26

13 The Legacy of John Adams 28

Timeline 30

Glossary 31

Index 32

Web Sites 32

Meet John Adams

Like George Washington and Thomas Jefferson, John Adams was an important Founding Father who helped shape the future of the United States. A leader in the American Revolution, he became the second president of the United States.

John Adams was born in Braintree, Massachusetts, in 1735. His father was a farmer and a deacon. Growing up, Adams was curious and liked to read books. He was honest and purposeful in all that he did. He was so purposeful in fact, that some people said he was very stubborn. Adams began studying to become a minister at Harvard College in 1751. He changed his mind after graduating from Harvard in 1755, and he later became a lawyer. When he was 23, he moved back to Braintree and began his law practice. During this time, hostilities in Boston were rising between colonists and the British government.

Colonists were upset with the taxes and laws that the British government imposed on them. Hostilities erupted in 1770 during the Boston Massacre. A small group of British soldiers shot into a mob of angry protesters, killing five colonists and wounding others. Although Adams supported the colonists, he defended the British soldiers charged with murder. Adams believed that everyone deserved a fair trial. After this event, the differences between the colonists and Britain grew, and Adams soon came to believe that the colonies should be independent of Britain.

You will need the following supplies to draw the life and times of John Adams:

✓ A sketch pad   ✓ An eraser   ✓ A pencil   ✓ A ruler

These are some of the shapes and drawing terms you need to know:

Horizontal Line	——	Squiggly Line	∿∿
Oval	⬭	Trapezoid	▱
Rectangle	▭	Triangle	△
Shading	▰	Vertical Line	|
Slanted Line	/	Wavy Line	∿

The Second President

When the American Revolution began in 1775, John Adams served in the Continental Congress. The Congress was the new, independent American government during the war against Britain. In 1776, Adams signed the Declaration of Independence.

In 1777, Congress selected Adams to serve as a diplomat. He would represent the interests of America in foreign countries, such as France and the Netherlands. In 1781, the Americans beat the British at Yorktown, Virginia. After this victory, Adams assisted in making the Treaty of Paris that ended the American Revolution. The treaty was signed in 1783.

After the Revolution, George Washington was elected the first president of the United States. Adams became the first vice president. When Washington retired after his second term, Adams was elected president in 1796. Adams encountered many problems while he was president, and he was not elected to serve a second term. Adams retired to his longtime home in Braintree, after having spent many long years serving his nation.

One of the issues Adams faced as president was the risk of war with France. After some problems, he was able to negotiate peace. This was one of his greatest accomplishments.

John Adams's Massachusetts

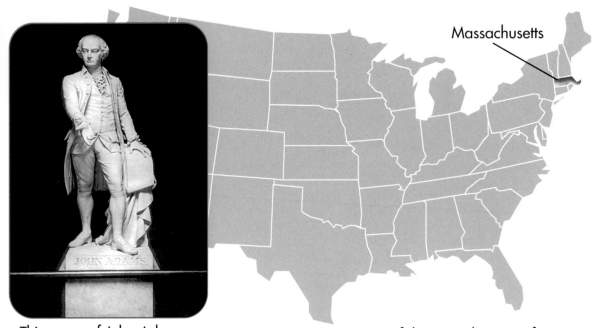

This statue of John Adams is part of the Harvard University Portrait Collection in Memorial Hall.

Massachusetts

Map of the United States of America

Today the area of Braintree where John Adams was born, and where he finally retired, is called Quincy. The Adams National Historical Park is in Quincy. The lands and houses in the park were home to five generations of the Adams family. The houses include the birthplace of both John Adams and John Quincy Adams. In the center of Quincy, the United First Parish Church holds the grave of Abigail and John Adams, who are buried side by side. Abigail Adams, John's wife, was born in nearby Weymouth, Massachusetts.

Many important events that led up to the American Revolution occurred in Boston, just 8 miles (12.9 km) north of Quincy. People in Massachusetts are very proud of their colonial history and the role Massachusetts played in forming the United States. The Freedom Trail is marked by a big orange line running through the streets and sidewalks of Boston. It provides a path to see many historic places. Along the trail, one can see the Old State House. It was built in 1713 to hold the colonial government of the British. Faneuil Hall is a market and meeting hall in the center of Boston where Adams may have attended a meeting or seen a protest. The city is known as the cradle of liberty. There is also a marble statue of Adams at Harvard University, in Cambridge, which was sculpted by Randolph Rogers in 1859.

Built in 1713, the Old State House is the oldest public building in Boston. After a speech there by James Otis in support of the American Revolution, John Adams wrote, "Then and there the child Independence was born."

Childhood and Family

Born in October 1735, John Adams was the first of three sons born to John Adams and Susanna Boylston Adams. Adams grew up in a

house with four rooms on a small farm. Farming in New England is hard because the weather is uncertain, and the growing season is short. Farmers like John Adams's parents did not have a lot of money, and they lived simply.

Growing up, Adams and his brothers would help their father with chores. They would also hunt, fish, and play outdoors. The boys also attended church with their parents. Many people in Massachusetts followed a type of Christian religion called Puritanism. Adams's thinking was founded on Puritan teachings of honesty, hard work, and plainness. For example, as a diplomat in France, Adams was shocked by the excesses of French food, clothing, and culture.

1

To begin drawing John Adams's childhood home, draw a long horizontal line that slopes slightly downward toward the left. On top of this, draw lines to make a square and a rectangle as shown.

2

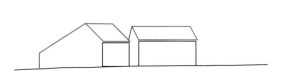

Draw slanted roofs on top of the houses. Add a short slanted line to the roof on the right. Add a long slanted line to the house on the left. Draw a vertical line from the line you have just drawn down to the horizontal line.

3

Add rectangles for the doors and the windows. Draw the shapes shown for the chimneys. There are two on the left building, and there is one on the right.

4

Add windows to the side of the house on the right. Add vertical lines to each side of the doorway. Draw a triangle at the top of these lines. In front of the house, add slanting lines and a short vertical line to begin stone walls.

5

Draw a long curvy line next to the stone wall. This will be where the grass is. Draw trees and bushes. Add lines to the windows. Draw lines to make a small triangle on top of the doorway of the house on the left.

6

Erase the lines of the wall that cross over the trees and bushes. Add as much detail to the drawing as you like. Finish with shading. See where the shading is darker in some parts than in others. Well done! You are finished.

The Education of John Adams

Adams wanted to become a farmer like his dad, but his father encouraged him to study to be a minister. At the age of 10, Adams went to a Latin school, which prepared children for college by teaching Latin, math, and

other advanced subjects. Adams did not like the classes because he did not like his teacher, and he wanted to be outside. Adams's studies improved when he began going to a new teacher, Joseph Marsh, who inspired Adams's lifelong love of reading and study.

Adams attended Harvard College from 1751 until 1755. When he attended Harvard, there were just 90 students in his class, and three brick buildings made up the whole campus, or grounds. When Adams went to Harvard, he was going to become a minister, as his father wanted. After his time at Harvard, however, Adams changed his mind and thought he might be a better lawyer. He enjoyed reading and debating. He met a lawyer who agreed to teach him law.

1

Begin drawing Harvard's seal by making a circle. This will be your guideline for the plants and banner. Draw a shield shape inside the circle. The top edges of the shield touch the circle.

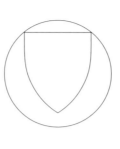

2

Draw a smaller shield shape inside the shield you just drew. Draw a curved line that follows the guide circle on the bottom. Draw two slanting lines on each end of the curved line. This shape will be the banner.

3

Draw two rectangles in the shield, as shown. One rectangle is longer than the other. Draw two more straight lines at the banner's edges. Add four circles at either end of the lines.

4

Draw more curved lines inside the guide circle. Notice how they do not cross over the shield. Add four more rough circles to the lines on the banner. Draw five vertical lines inside the rectangles on the shield.

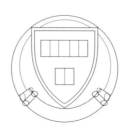

5

Erase the center part of the top rectangle leaving two sets of rectangles with space between them. Draw rectangles around the rectangle pairs. You are making little books. Erase extra lines around the banner. Now the banner has curvy edges. Write "HARVARD" in capital letters.

6

Write "VERITAS" in the boxes as shown. Veritas means "truth" in Latin. Add ovals, rectangles, and tiny curved shapes around the sides of the books. Draw curvy lines inside the shapes at the edges of the banner. Begin to draw the shapes for the leaves that will circle the shield.

7

Erase the lines that run through the small shapes around the edges of the books. Erase part of the line behind the A in the bottom book. Finish drawing the leaves, using the circles as guidelines. Try to make the plants match on each side.

8

Erase the guidelines. You can finish your drawing with shading. Notice how there is no shading where the letters are written. Good job!

Love and Marriage

In 1758, when John Adams was 23, he moved back to Braintree and set up his own law practice. He gained a reputation as an excellent lawyer, and his law practice grew.

In 1759, Adams met Abigail Smith for the first time. A friend of Adams's was seeing Abigail's sister Mary. John and Abigail fell in love and were married in 1764. Abigail was smart and had an independent spirit. She believed that women should be educated just as men were. Abigail often served as Adams's adviser. She and John were apart for many years of their marriage, but the letters they wrote to each other show Abigail's advice and intelligence. The bond between John and Abigail Adams was strong, and he often called her his partner and best friend.

John and Abigail had five children. One of their sons, John Quincy Adams, born in 1767, grew up to become the sixth president of the United States.

1
Draw a rectangle. Inside the rectangle, draw a long oval that tilts slightly to the right. Add a curved line to the side of the oval. Draw a vertical guideline for the neck and the body.

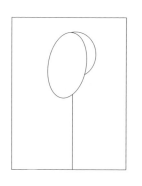

2
Draw a horizontal line across the vertical line you just drew. This will be a guide for the shoulders. Add an oval for the ear. Draw lines inside the large oval. These will be your guides for drawing the eyes, nose, and mouth.

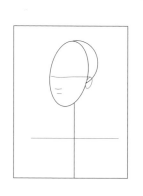

3
Draw lines for the side of the face and for the outline of Abigail's hair. Draw small curved lines inside the ear. Add ovals for the eyes. Draw the lines for the eyebrows. Erase any extra lines.

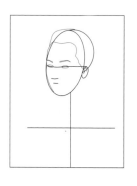

4
Erase parts of the head guidelines and the eye guideline. Add details to the eyes. Draw the nose and the mouth. Draw the outline of the neck, shoulders, and arm, as shown.

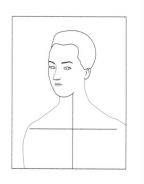

5
Erase the nose and the mouth guidelines. Erase the guidelines for the body. Add dots inside the eyes. Draw three rows of tiny circles for the necklace. Add ribbons for the hair.

6
Looking at the photograph on the opposite page and at the drawing shown here, add the many lines for the clothing. Erase the part of the neck that goes through the necklace circles.

7
Erase the lines of the shoulders that pass through the clothing. Finish with shading. Notice how the background shading on the left is darker than the shading on the right. Well done! You have just drawn a picture of Abigail Adams.

The Stamp Act

Between 1754 and 1763, the British fought against the French and several Native American nations for control of land in America. The war cost the British government a lot of money. The British wanted the colonists to help pay for it. The Stamp Act of 1765, which placed a tax on items such as newspapers and legal documents, was an example of the taxes the British used to raise money. The colonists felt that they paid enough taxes. They were against the Stamp Act and refused to pay the new taxes. They made such items as the teapot shown here in protest.

Adams was included in the action. Many of his clients were merchants who fought new taxes in the courts. Adams saw that the differences between Britain and the colonies were very deep. Tensions rose, and in March 1770, the Boston Massacre occurred. The massacre, shown above, left the colonists even angrier with the British government than they had been before.

1

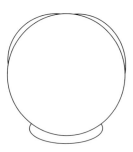

Now we're going to draw the teapot! Draw a circle. Add two curved lines to the top. Add the curvy shape to the bottom.

2

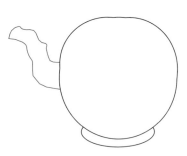

Erase the lines of the circle that are beneath the two curves at the top of the teapot. Draw the squiggly shape on the left side to make the spout of the teapot.

3

Draw a small curved line at the top of the spout. Add the handle. Draw the rectangular shape with rounded corners inside the teapot. Write "No Stamp Act" in the shape.

4

Add the shapes for the knob at the top. Draw the design at the front of the teapot as shown. Don't forget the squiggly lines near the words.

5

Continue to draw the rest of the design around the curved rectangular guideline.

6

Erase the guideline. Finish the design by adding the shapes to the top of the teapot.

7

You can finish your teapot with shading. Use the photograph on page 16 to help you. Well done.

The American Revolution

In 1773, colonists dumped British tea into Boston Harbor to protest a tax on tea. This event was known as the Boston Tea

Party. The British then shut down the port of Boston, and most business in the city came to a halt. Representatives from each of the colonies were chosen to discuss how to react. These representatives met in the First Continental Congress of 1774. The colonists in Massachusetts chose John Adams to represent them.

The colonies decided to prepare for a possible war with Britain. British soldiers fought with a local militia in Lexington, Massachusetts, in the spring of 1775. This was the beginning of the American Revolution. The attack on Massachusetts colonists, and their successful defense of it, only strengthened the will of Adams and the colonists. "Don't Tread on Me" and other slogans became cries of the Revolution. On July 4, 1776, John Adams and other members of the Continental Congress signed the Declaration of Independence.

1

You are now going to draw a poster from the Revolution. Begin by drawing a long spiral. It has three loops. This spiral will be your guide for drawing the snake's body.

2

DONT TREAD ON ME

Add an oval guideline for the head. Write "DON'T TREAD ON ME" in capital letters beneath the snake guides.

3

DONT TREAD ON ME

Draw the lines inside the oval as shown. These lines will be the snake's open mouth. Begin to draw the body by adding the lines around the first loop.

4

DONT TREAD ON ME

Erase the oval guideline. Erase the part of the body guideline that runs between the lines you just drew. Add more curvy lines for the middle part of the body.

5

DONT TREAD ON ME

Erase the central guideline of the middle part of the body. Draw more lines toward the bottom part of the body. Add lines for the eyes, nose, and tongue. Draw a sharp tooth.

6

DONT TREAD ON ME

Erase the central guideline inside the lines you just drew. Draw the tail. Draw a long rough rectangle for the flag. Add two small circles to the left side of the flag and a rough vertical line at the edge.

7

DONT TREAD ON ME

Erase the remaining guideline. Look carefully at the drawing and add the shapes to the snake's body. Many of them are triangles. Draw small curved lines on the tail. Draw a small curved line near the head for the jaw.

8

DONT TREAD ON ME

Add lines for the grass beneath the snake. Finish with shading. You can use the side of your pencil tip to shade the flag lightly. Well done! You did a great job.

John Adams Becomes a Diplomat

Although America had declared independence, the war continued with Britain. In 1777, Congress sent Adams to Paris, France, to work on an alliance, or friendship, with France. He traveled there in a  ship called the *Boston*. When he arrived, however, the alliance with France had already been accomplished. In 1779, Adams sailed home to be with his family.

The life of the diplomat was not over for Adams, however. He returned to France in 1780 to negotiate a treaty to end the war with Britain. The French made the negotiations hard, and talks happened slowly. Feeling let down, Adams went to the Netherlands to try to gain that country as an ally. While he was there, the colonists and their French allies beat the British at Yorktown in 1781. After securing a loan and promise of friendship from the Netherlands in 1782, Adams returned to France. He helped negotiate the Treaty of Paris, which was signed in 1783. This treaty officially ended the American Revolution.

1

Begin by drawing the body of the boat. Notice how the lines are uneven. Draw a rough line for the water under the boat.

2

Use a ruler to draw the poles as shown. Make sure the ends of the poles are pointed, as they are here. Do not forget about the short pole coming from the right side of the boat. There are five poles in total.

3

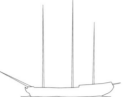

Add the horizontal shapes across the three middle poles. Draw a rough horizontal line on the right side. Add details to either end of the boat. Draw small circles and shapes for the windows along the side of the boat.

4

Draw the small straight lines in the middle of the boat. Look at the drawing carefully and begin to draw the sails. Draw a flag and its pole. Draw ropes on the right.

5

Look at the drawing carefully and add five more sails, as shown. Notice how they overlap. Next draw a slanted line going across the front pole.

6

Add the lines to the slanted line you just drew. These lines are to show a folded sail. Add more pointed sails and straight lines to the front of the boat. Draw small rectangles on the three middle poles.

7

Add a flag to the center pole. Draw slanted lines at the top of the three center poles. Use a ruler to add lines for ropes coming from the poles and sails. Draw a rough line near the bottom of the boat.

8

You can add as much detail to the boat as you like. Finish with shading. Look closely at the shading. See how the sails cast shadows on some of the other sails.

First Vice President of the United States

In the years following the American Revolution, Adams continued his duties as a diplomat. In 1788, after almost a decade of foreign service, he returned home to his farm. However, quiet time with his family would not last for long. In February 1789, the war hero George Washington was

FEDERAL HALL
The Seat of Congress

elected the first president of the United States. John Adams was elected the first vice president. The president and vice president took office in Federal Hall in New York City on April 21, 1789.

As vice president, Adams was not popular with his fellow politicians. He spoke his mind often, but not everybody agreed with him. As a result, Adams's role as a member of Washington's cabinet of advisers was limited. In fact, Adams felt he was doing so little, he famously complained that he felt that the role of the vice president was "insignificant," or not important.

1

To begin Federal Hall, draw a large rectangle. Draw a horizontal line at the bottom of the rectangle. Draw another rectangle that sits on this line.

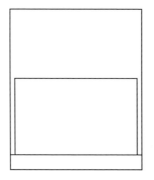

2

Draw a long vertical line in the center of the large rectangle. Draw lines for a a roof as shown. Draw small rectangles on top of the roof for the tower.

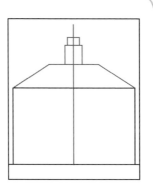

3

Add curved lines at the top of the building. Draw two slanted lines in the roof, so that they make a triangle. Add horizontal and vertical lines to the front of the building.

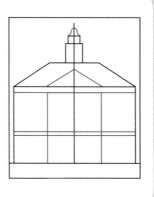

4

Add vertical shapes to either side of the roof, as shown. These are chimneys. Add more lines to the front of the building. Draw eight rectangles for windows.

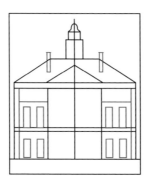

5

Erase extra lines. Add lines for the tips of two more chimneys. Add a circle and lines to the roof. Add a circle, an arch, and a dot to the tower. Add windows and columns to the building, as shown.

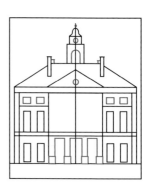

6

Add more details to the tower. Draw two more slanted lines to make another triangle in the roof. Draw small lines at the sides of the roof. Add columns and detail to the front of the building.

7

Erase extra lines. Add the bird shape around the circle inside the triangle. Look at the picture and the photograph carefully, and add details to the rest of the building.

8

Add more details and shading to finish. Notice how the doorways are dark. Well done! You have finished drawing Federal Hall in New York City.

Peace with France

When Washington retired from politics, Adams was elected president. When he took office in 1797, the British and the French were at war.  Both countries attacked U.S. ships and caused problems for American businesses. Groups in America pressured Adams to support France or Britain.

Adams sent diplomats to France in 1798 to negotiate peace. The French refused to see the Americans without being paid a bribe. The event, shown above, was called the XYZ Affair, because the French agents were known as X, Y, and Z.

Adams and Congress prepared for war against France. The risk of war was enough to make the French government willing to talk with the Americans without a bribe. Adams sent ministers to France and was able to avoid a war. Adams believed that keeping the peace with France was one of his greatest accomplishments.

1

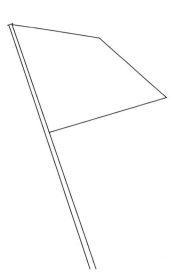

You are going to draw the French flag. Begin by using your ruler to draw two slanted lines, as shown. These will be your flagpole. Draw a small line at the top of the flagpole. Next draw three slanted lines coming from the flagpole, as shown. These are your guides for drawing the flag.

2

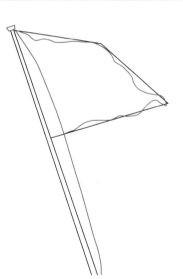

Draw a small trapezoid at the top of the flagpole. Draw a long, slightly curved line to the right of the flagpole. This is a rope. Inside the guidelines you drew in the last step, draw the curvy lines for the flag, as shown. You can use the photograph on the opposite page to help you.

3

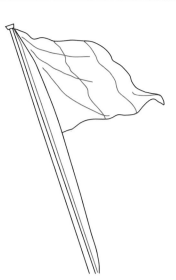

Erase the flag guide shape. Draw two wavy vertical lines on the flag. Draw three curved lines coming from the top left corner. These lines will create ripples in the flag. Add another long, slightly curved line for another rope.

4

Finish your flag with shading. Start by shading in the flagpole. Next shade the three different sections of the flag. The first will be very dark, the next will be the lightest, and the last will be somewhere between the two. These sections stand for the blue, white, and red colors on the French flag.

The Presidential Election of 1800

Maintaining peace with France, however, would cost Adams the presidency. Adams belonged to a political party called the Federalists. They believed a strong central government

would make America strong. Party members were divided over whether to go to war with France, and other policies. As a result, many Federalists did not support Adams in the 1800 election. Instead the Republican candidate, Thomas Jefferson, was elected president. The Republican Party believed in giving more power to the states.

Before Jefferson took office in 1801, Adams moved into the White House in the new capital city of Washington, D.C. He was the first president to occupy the White House. On his second night there, John Adams wrote to Abigail, saying, "May none but honest and wise Men ever rule under this roof." These words are now carved on the wall of the State Dining Room in the White House.

1

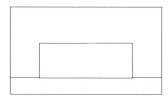

To draw the White House, begin by drawing a large rectangle. Draw a horizontal line at the bottom of the rectangle. Add a rectangle that sits on top of this line.

2

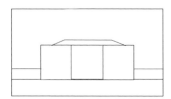

Draw two horizontal lines on either side of the small rectangle. Inside this rectangle, draw straight lines to make a square. Draw a horizontal line, with two slanted lines at each end to make the roof.

3

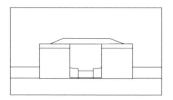

The smaller rectangle now has three sections. In the middle section, add the lines to make three shapes, as shown. In the outer two sections, draw horizontal lines near the top.

4

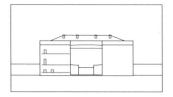

Draw four small chimneys on the roof. Draw two horizontal lines near the top of the middle section. Draw three horizontal lines in the left section. Add four shapes, as shown, for windows.

5

Erase extra lines. Draw four horizontal lines, two on each side of the building. Add small curvy tops to the chimneys. Add three horizontal lines in the right section of the building. Finish drawing the windows.

6

Erase the window guidelines. Add small columns to the sides of the building. Add columns to the center section, as well. Add two arches for doors. Draw a row of thin rectangles on the top of the building.

7

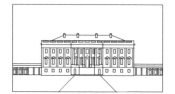

Add two tiny lines on either side of the building near the roof. Add the details to all three sections of the building. Add shapes between the columns. Draw two slanted lines in front of the building.

8

You can finish your drawing with shading. Some places need darker shading than others. Notice the shadow that runs from the center to the right side. Well done. You have just drawn the White House!

The Legacy of John Adams

The always honest and plainspoken Adams returned home to Massachusetts after his term ended. He felt bitterly let down by his loss in the reelection campaign. Adams continued to write about politics in letters to his friends and to his son John Quincy.

Adams also began to write to Jefferson after the War of 1812. On July 4, 1826, John Adams died in his bed, on the same day as Jefferson. It was 50 years after the signing of the Declaration of Independence.

Adams spent many years serving his country as a representative, as a diplomat during the American Revolution, and later as president. He was responsible for writing the constitution of the new state of Massachusetts, which was completed in 1779. This would later become one of the models of the U.S. Constitution. This is one of John Adams's many accomplishments that live on in America today.

1

Draw a rectangle. Inside the rectangle, draw an oval. Add a curved line to the side of the oval. These are guides for you to draw John Adams's head. Draw a vertical guideline for the neck and the body.

2

Draw the guidelines for the eyes, the nose, and the mouth. Draw the outlines for the neck and the arms.

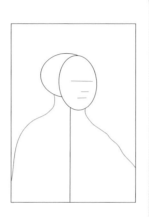

3

Erase the vertical guideline. Draw curvy lines for the face and the jaw, as shown. Draw ovals for the eyes. Draw the eyebrows. Draw a small curved line at the nose guideline. Draw lines for the mouth.

4

Erase the guidelines for the eyes and the mouth. Erase part of the head oval, as shown. Draw more lines around the eyes. Add circles inside the eyes. Add a line for the nose. Draw squiggly lines for the hair, using the guide to help you.

5

Erase the nose and the head guidelines. Add dots to the center of the eyes. Draw lines for the jacket, the shirt, and the hair ribbon at the back of the collar, as shown.

6

Erase extra lines. Add details to the hair and shirt, as shown. You can finish your picture of John Adams with shading. Notice in particular the shading around the face area. Notice, too, that the shading is darker in some parts. Well done! You are finished.

Timeline

1732   George Washington is born on February 22.

1735   John Adams is born.

1764   John Adams and Abigail Smith are married.

1770   Adams defends the British soldiers accused of murder during the Boston Massacre.

1775   The American Revolution begins.

1776   The Declaration of Independence is signed.

1777   Congress sends Adams to France as a diplomat.

1779   Adams drafts the Massachusetts Constitution.

1780   Adams returns to Paris as a diplomat in France and later in the Netherlands.

1781   The Americans defeat the British at Yorktown.

1783   America and Britain sign the Treaty of Paris.

1789   George Washington is elected the first president, and John Adams becomes vice president.

1796   John Adams is elected president.

1798   The XYZ Affair happens in France.

1799   Adams avoids war with France.

1800   Adams moves into the White House.

1801   Thomas Jefferson takes office as president.

1826   John Adams and Thomas Jefferson die on the fiftieth anniversary of America's independence.

Glossary

agents (AY-jents) People who act for another.

American Revolution (uh-MER-uh-ken reh-vuh-LOO-shun) Battles that soldiers from the colonies fought against Britain for freedom, from 1775 to 1783.

bribe (BRYB) Money or a favor given in return for something else.

Continental Congress (kon-tih-NEN-tul KON-gres) A group, made up of a few people from every colony, that made decisions for the colonies.

culture (KUL-chur) The beliefs, practices, and arts of a group of people.

deacon (DEE-kun) An officer of the church.

debating (dih-BAYT-ing) Arguing or discussing.

Declaration of Independence (deh-kluh-RAY-shun UV in-duh-PEN-dints) An official announcement in which American colonists stated they were free of British rule.

defended (dih-FEND-ed) Took someone's side in an argument.

diplomat (DIH-pluh-mat) A person who represents his or her country's interest in a foreign country.

excesses (EK-ses-ez) Amounts greater than what is needed or usual.

foreign (FOR-in) Outside one's own country.

lawyer (LOY-er) Someone who gives advice about the law.

legacy (LEH-guh-see) Something that has been handed down from another person.

massacre (MA-sih-ker) The act of killing a large number of people or animals.

militia (muh-LIH-shuh) A group of people who are trained to fight when needed.

negotiate (nih-GOH-shee-ayt) To talk over and arrange terms for an agreement.

policies (PAH-lih-seez) Laws that people use to help them make decisions.

react (ree-AKT) To act because something has happened.

reputation (reh-pyoo-TAY-shun) The ideas people have about another person, an animal, or an object.

smuggled (SMUH-guld) Sneaked something banned into the country.

stubborn (STUH-burn) Wanting to have one's own way.

tensions (TEN-shunz) The uneasiness between two groups of people or things.

Index

A

Adams, Abigail, 8, 14, 26,

Adams, John (father), 10

Adams, John Quincy, 8, 14, 28

Adams, Susanna Boylston (mother), 10

Adams National Historical Park, 8

American Revolution, 4, 6, 9, 18, 20, 22, 28

B

Boston, Massachusetts, 9, 18, 20

Boston Massacre, 5, 16

Boston Tea Party, 18

Braintree, Massachusetts, 4, 6, 8, 14

C

Constitution, United States, 28

Continental Congress, 6, 18, 20

D

Declaration of Independence, 6, 18, 28

F

Faneuil Hall, 9

Federal Hall, 22

France, 6, 10, 20, 24

Freedom Trail, 9

H

Harvard College, 4, 9, 12,

J

Jefferson, Thomas, 4, 26, 28

M

Marsh, Joseph, 12

N

Netherlands, the, 6

O

Old State House, 9

P

Puritanism, 10

Q

Quincy, Massachusetts, 8,

R

Rogers, Randolph, 9

S

Stamp Act, 16

T

Treaty of Paris, 6, 20

W

Washington, George, 4, 6, 22, 24

White House, 26

X

XYZ Affair, 24

Web Sites

Due to the changing nature of Internet links, PowerKids Press has developed an online list of Web sites related to the subject of this book. This site is updated regularly. Please use this link to access the list:

www.powerkidslinks.com/KGDPUSA/adams/